MINING SCHOOLS

IN THE

UNITED STATES.

BY

JOHN A. CHURCH, E. M.

Reprinted (by permission) from the North American Review for January, 1871, at the request of the Trustees of Columbia College.

New York:
WALDRON & PAYNE, Printers.
1871.

SCHOOL OF MINES,
COLUMBIA COLLEGE.

FACULTY

F. A. P. BARNARD, S.T.D., LL.D., PRESIDENT.

T. EGGLESTON, JR., E.M.,	Mineralogy and Metallurgy.
FRANCIS L. VINTON, E.M.,	Mining Engineering.
C. F. CHANDLER, PH.D.,	Analytical and Applied Chemistry.
JOHN TORREY, M.D., LL.D.,	Botany.
CHARLES A. JOY, PH.D.,	General Chemistry.
WILLIAM G. PECK, LL.D.,	Mechanics.
JOHN H. VAN AMRINGE, A.M.,	Mathematics.
OGDEN N. ROOD, A.M.,	Physics.
JOHN S. NEWBERRY, M.D., LL.D.,	Geology and Paleontology.

ASSISTANTS.

JOHN HENRY CASWELL, A.B.,	Mineralogy.
ALBERT FOLKE, C.E.,	Drawing.
ALEXIS A. JULIEN, A.M.,	Analytical Chemistry.
WILLIAM H. CHANDLER,	Analytical Chemistry.
PAUL SCHWEITZER, PH.D.,	Analytical Chemistry.
THOMAS M. BLOSSOM, A.M., E.M.	Assaying.
W. B. POTTER, A.M., E.M.,	Geology.
HENRY NEWTON, E.M.,	Metallurgy.
DOUGLAS A. JOY,	General Chemistry.
EDWARD C. H. DAY,	Registrar.

There are five regular three year courses of instruction for the degree of Engineer of Mines, or Bachelor of Philosophy, viz.:

I. CIVIL ENGINEERING. II. MINING ENGINEERING.
III. METALLURGY. IV. GELOGOY AND NATURAL HISTORY.
V. ANALYTICAL AND APPLIED CHEMISTRY.

There is a Supplementary year of instruction for the degree of Doctor of Philosophy. There is a preparatory year for those not qualified for the regular courses.

Requirements for Admission.—Candidates for a degree must be at least eighteen years of age, and must pass a satisfactory examination in algebra, geometry, plane, analytical and spherical trigonometry.

Graduates of Colleges and Schools of science whose course of study is equivalent to the requirements for admission, may be admitted to the first year as regular students, on presenting their diplomas, without examination.

Candidates for advanced standing are examined in all the studies previously pursued by the classes which they propose to enter.

Candidates for the preparatory year must be seventeen years of age, and must pass a satisfactory examination in arithmetic, including the metric system of weights, measures and moneys; in algebra through simple equations; and in geometry, on the first four books of Davies' Legendre.

Special students, not candidates for a degree, may pursue any of the branches taught in the school, without previous examination.

Expenses.—The fee for the full course, including instruction, use of laboratories, apparatus, chemicals, drawing-room, and students' collection of minerals, is $200 per annum.

For special students in Chemistry and Assaying the fee is $200.

Special students in Assaying are admitted for two months for a fee of $50.

For single courses of lectures the fees vary from $10 to $30.

Pecuniary aid is extended to those not able to meet the expenses of the school.

The next year begins October 2d, 1871. The examinations for admissions will be held on Thursday, September 28th, 1871.

For further information and for catalogues, apply to

Dr. C. F. CHANDLER, Dean of the Faculty.

East 49th Street, New York.

MINING SCHOOLS

IN THE

UNITED STATES.

BY

JOHN A. CHURCH, E. M.

Reprinted (by permission) from the North American Review for January, 1871, at the request of the Trustees of Columbia College.

New York:
WALDRON & PAYNE, Printers.
1871.

INTRODUCTION.

COLUMBIA COLLEGE,
New York, February 11, 1871.

JOHN A. CHURCH, Esq.:

Dear Sir—The article upon Mining Education prepared by you for the "North American Review," and published in the January number of that journal for the current year, presents so complete and clear a view of the state of this important department of technical education, abroad and at home, and especially of the wants of our own country in respect to it, and of the provisions which have been thus far made to supply them, as to induce the belief that it ought to receive a wider circulation than it is likely to secure in the pages of the "Review."

The trustees of Columbia College, under whose auspices was founded, a little more than six years ago, the first school of Mining Science erected in this country, and the only one in which as yet this branch of education has been made the principal, as it was originally the exclusive, object, have been gratified that, in your historical sketch, you have done justice to their efforts. They have spared no expense in bringing together here all the instrumentalities necessary or desirable for imparting instruction in the several branches of mathematical, mechanical, physical, and chemical science, and the applications of those sciences to mine engineering, to metallurgy, and to civil and dynamical engineering. They have employed professors whose ability is attested not only by their own well-established reputation, but by the honorable success of the graduates formed under their teaching. They have aimed, and as they believe successfully, to establish here a system of education in which practice shall be as largely as possible combined with theory. It is believed that there is no school of applied science in the country which is sustained at so large an annual expense as this. It is, of course, not sustained by the fees received from its students for tuition. These have never exceeded, and perhaps have hardly equaled, the third part of its disbursements. It is no part of its plan that it should be self-sustaining. On the other hand, it has admitted many students, and continues to admit students, when circumstances justify, free of all charge for tuition.

The school has thus already contributed, to an important degree, and it is contributing more and more largely every year, to provide a class of men greatly needed in our country for the intelligent development of some of the richest sources of our natural wealth, for increasing the productiveness of such as have been productive, and for drawing profit from others which wasteful ignorance has hitherto attempted only with loss and disaster. It is only necessary that the character of this institution shall become known to those who are interested in the mining and metallurgic industry of our country, that its advantages may be appreciated and its usefulness largely extended. And it is the belief of the trustees that, by the republication and extensive circulation of your article above mentioned, something may be done to convey this knowledge to those whom it might benefit, and through whose benefit the country may be benefited likewise.

The trustees therefore authorize and instruct me to inquire whether you are willing to allow a reprint of the article referred to, to be made for their use.

I have the honor to be, dear sir,

Your obedient servant,

F. A. P. BARNARD,
President of Columbia College.

Office of the Army and Navy Journal,
New York, February 13, 1871.

Dr. F. A. P. Barnard, President of Columbia College:

Dear Sir—Your kind letter of the 11th is received. I shall be pleased to have the article on Mining Schools republished by the trustees of Columbia College, and more pleased if it prove of any value to the cause of intelligent mining in this country, or to the profession of mining engineering.

I am, with great respect,

Yours,

JOHN A. CHURCH.

MINING SCHOOLS

IN

THE UNITED STATES.

IN the year 1714 the English Parliament offered the sum of twenty thousand pounds to the discoverer of any means by which the captain of a ship at sea could determine his position on the ocean within thirty miles. Not even this shining reward—the greatest, perhaps, ever offered for a scientific discovery, and at that time a fortune in itself—could effect the object. A method was proposed, but the committee to which it was referred declared that no astronomical tables existed of sufficient correctness to make it of any value. With the best data the world then possessed, the error might be as great as nine hundred miles; * and to bring it down even to two hundred miles, an extensive series of new observations of the heavenly bodies must be undertaken. Charles II., to whom the report was made, is said to have exclaimed on reading the letter, "But I must have them observed;" and he thereupon founded the Observatory at Greenwich, an institution to which every nation that has a marine owes an incalculable debt for the commercial prosperity it enjoys, and upon which the sailor in every clime depends for the safety and certainty with which he traverses the ocean. From thirty per cent. per voyage—the rate of insurance when Greece was in her glory—to the two and three per cent. which is now current, the decrease of the expenses of

* F. A. P. Barnard, LL.D., S.T.D., in his Letter to the Board of Trustees of the University of Mississippi, 1858.

commerce has kept perfect time with the march of scientific investigation and the founding of seats of scientific learning.

Our own country presents to-day an example of the dependence of industry upon knowledge which is quite as remarkable as that given above. Commissioner Ross Browne, in his report on our Western mines, says that experienced investors in mining property will not pay for a mine more than two and a half times its yearly profit. That is to say, they do not consider it a safe investment unless it returns *forty per cent.* upon its cost.* The reason of this is plain. With no means of educating miners to their work, the conduct of mines in this country is a lamentable story of mismanagement, energy wrongly directed, and consequent great losses. The thousand millions of gold dollars that have been won from the ground in California are but an inadequate representation of the real wealth that existed there.† Observers have estimated the losses which were at first caused by ignorant and hasty methods of working at *two thirds* of the gold really at hand, and none have put them at less than one half. A better state of affairs has gradually grown up, but the losses to this day are very much larger than they should be. In California, however,

* It is, of course, difficult to obtain accurate information of the market value of mines, as the calculations are almost always kept private and estimates based upon problematical cases are not entirely trustworthy. Still, in looking over the report of the mining commissioner for 1871, I find one case mentioned—the only case in the whole book which gives the figures necessary for a calculation—which offers a basis for a very extraordinary exhibition of the different value a mine has in ignorant and in educated hands. The mine is reported to show a heavy deposit of lead ore containing silver to the amount of $400 a ton, and it is yielding 55 tons a day; daily value of yield, therefore, $22,000. The cost of smelting precisely similar ores in the same valley is given at $20 a ton; *maximum* cost of mining, $5 a ton; daily cost of mining and smelting 55 tons of ore, therefore, $1,375; difference, $20,625. Allowing a loss of three per cent. upon this, we have a daily profit of $20,000. The mine was sold for precisely that sum—$20,000. Smelting works could have been built for $40,000, so that the mine would pay for itself and its smelting works *twice a week* as long as its present yield continues. I do not give this as a calculation minutely correct, but it certainly is an instance of a mine whose real value greatly exceeded its market price; and whose real value would probably have been obtained had its owner sought the aid of an experienced man.

† Bullion product of California, 1849-1869	$948,000,000
" " of other States up to 1869	315,000,000
—*Report on Mines*, 1871.	$1,263,000,000

the work has been easy to that called for by more difficult ores in Nevada, Montana and Colorado; and if an investigation could be had of the exact proportion of precious metal saved to the quantity in the ore, the story would be astonishing even to scientific men. Without careful proof it is impossible to make men believe the reports of the few competent observers who have been there, so apparently incredible are the results of recklessness and want of knowledge. It was difficult to introduce even the thinnest entering-wedge of common sense into this hard prejudice against skill and study. For a long time the miners refused all help from schools or scholars; but the experience of continual trouble with their ores, and the gradually developed fact that they often lost more than they gained, have worked a complete revolution. A beginning having been made in New York in 1864, a number of schools of mines, more or less praiseworthy, have been founded in various parts of the United States. In Europe schools of this kind are among the oldest institutions of advanced learning, and our educators naturally look to them as the models upon which our own constructions must be shaped. It is proposed in this paper to point out their peculiarities, and to discuss the requirements of similar schools in this country.

Like all other educational institutions, schools of mines in Europe form part of the system of government; but unlike the others, their officers, instead of belonging to the department of education, are connected with that of mines. That is to say, schools of this class are regarded as investments which are necessary to make mining either profitable or possible. To the knowledge of which they are the source the mines of Europe are indebted for their ability to work low-grade ores; and were that knowledge to be now eliminated and the world thrown back to its resources of a century ago, hundreds of mines would have to be given up, and bread would be taken from a hundred thousand mouths.

Three kinds of schools are found—primary, middle, and high schools or academies. The lower schools are among the most peculiar and interesting institutions for education in the world. Wherever there are government mining works of importance, and in some of the great private works, schools are established for teaching workmen of a certain grade the secrets of their calling. They are called in Germany *Bergschüle*, in contradistinction to the high-grade schools, which always bear the name *Bergakademie.*

The teachers employed in them are the officers of the works, who usually devote two hours on two or three days in each week to giving plain but strictly scientific explanations of the operations which go on in the furnaces, and of methods of attack in the mine. The nature of the studies followed naturally depends upon the occupation of the scholar. Those who work in the mines receive instruction in mining alone; and this instruction, instead of being general and intended to fit the learner for the practice of all kinds of mining, is altogether special, and confined pretty closely to work in mines of the kind in which he is employed.

So, too, in the metallurgical department, the instructor makes no effort to lay down a full course of metallurgy, but aims to make his hearers understand the furnaces at which they daily labor, the nature of the chemical changes produced, the method of dealing with accidents, exact details of construction, and the like. Thus, instead of being eclectic and scientific, the instruction is confined to imparting the traditions of the particular establishment to which the school is attached. In this system we have one cause of that remarkable conservation of distinct methods of treatment which, until late years, has been so great a hindrance to German metallurgy, and has prevented the study and adoption in one quarter of improvements made in another.

Still, the information gained in these places is a great advance on ignorance, pure and simple; and these schools are as much above nothingness as the *Bergakademien*, the centres of science and research, are above them. The listeners to these lectures are men who, having had in their youth the *minimum* of education required by law, have, in a long course of severe manual labor, lost almost all trace of what little scientific or general information they ever gained. It is a long ladder by which a man climbs up to a position in which he has the right to attend these lectures. Entering a metallurgical work, a young man first spends two or three years in wheeling slag to the waste-heap; then as much more time at each of the following steps: wheeling ore to the mixing-bed, shovelling ore into the weighing-bucket, weighing ore, work at the roasting heaps, throwing ore into the furnace. Here his progress is slower, and he may remain at the last employment five or ten years. Finally he becomes smelter or tapper of the furnace. The uneducated man can rise no higher. The educated man spends much less time at each of these grades, but go through them he must. He is usually occupied two or three years in all at the practical work, and then performs clerical duties in the office. Rising higher and higher, he may in time become director of a smelting establishment or a mining district. The director of the world-famous mines around Clausthal, Andreasberg, and Altenau, in the Upper Harz Mountains, is an instance of a man who has passed through the commonest grades of service to a high position; he was a picker of ore in his boyhood. Plattner, a thorough chemist, founder of the analysis with the blowpipe, and an elegant as well as scientific writer on metallurgical chemistry, began in the same way.

Schools of this primary class are composed of the educated and uneducated men, who have been fellow-workmen in the same mine, at the same furnace; but the former sit in the rostrum, the latter on the benches. The classes are composed of men who have spent fifteen to twenty-five years in the most trying manual labor. The refinements of science, if explained to them, would fall on dull ears. But they have been familiar all their lives with certain phenomena of the bowels of the earth, or others of intensely heated furnaces, and these things they are interested in and can learn about. A simple course in the rudiments of chemistry, physics, machines, and mining engineering, with more careful explanations of that particular portion of these arts which comes under their own observation, teaches them to go about their work understandingly, and to lay aside that vague fear, which the untaught often have in the presence of great and, to them, mysterious operations of nature or of art.* It adds also greatly to their efficiency as workmen, and their safety in circumstances of danger.

In these remarks on this lowest grade of mining schools, I desire to be far from underrating the value and ability of the lecturers. In small and obscure mountain towns men are found who, in the

* This is no unimportant consideration. German miners of all grades are exceedingly superstitious, and retain even now, after a century or two of schooling, some of the observances which in old times were a part of their daily life. Martin Luther's confident belief in a personal devil may be attributed to the traditions learned in his youth in the Mansfield mining region. His father was a common miner at a time when the fact that mines were the abode of unseen and impish spirits was undisputed. In Saxony, to-day, the miners would be alarmed as well as offended if any one were to descend the mine in any but the traditional costume; and with many, the salutation *Glück Auf* is given with religious care whenever a comrade is met in the passages of the mine. Such men require the most practical and plainest teaching.

midst of incessant physical and administrative labor, have kept up with the march of science, and taken care not only to make the its latest truths known to their hearers, but also to apply them in the conduct of the works under their charge. Applied science owes to them some of the most remarkable discoveries that have been made; and they may fairly be said to have done more than their brethren of the closet in developing arts, which besides a knowledge of science in its theory require also a minute conversance with its practice. Von Born, Augustin, and Ziervogel, whose labors in one branch of metallurgy—that of the extraction of silver—have been so valuable, were all directors of works.

The next grade of school is one where young men, the sons of miners or smelters, and who may or may not have been employed in their boyhood in the works, obtain a higher kind of instruction. They are not, as are the learners in the lower school, mere workmen, but may rise to any height, though their future is usually that of overseers or directors of small works. These institutions are still called *Bergschüle;* but the student spends all his time at study, is instructed in general mineralogy, metallurgy, chemistry, etc. Indeed, his own abilities are the only boundary to his advance. Often the successful student wins the prize of a year or two at an *Akademie*, and has the advantage of a thorough scientific education.

These two varieties of schools are united, as at Eisleben and Halle in Prussia, Chemnitz in Hungary, Pribram in Bohemia, etc.; or only the first kind is found, as at Agordo in Italy, Waldenberg in Silesia, and many other places. Finally, one or both will be found united with a great *Bergakademie*, as at Freiberg and at Clausthal. Russia, where everything is supposed to be perfect in system, has one *Bergakademie*, ten first-class and a hundred second-class *Bergschüle*. Prussia has two *Akademien*, two first-class and ten second-class *Schüle*. The other states of Europe have also taken similar care to educate their miners of all grades.

Of the mining academies four may be considered as of first rank. They are those of Paris, Freiberg in Saxony, Berlin, and St. Petersburg.* Austria, though far from lacking in good schools, has none of this grade, for a reason which will be given further on.

---

* The schools and academies of Sweden I am obliged to omit, as I have not seen them. Their reputation is, however, very great, and the academy at Stockholm should perhaps be added to the four mentioned above as belonging to the first rank.

These institutions, though working in the same field and giving instruction upon the same subjects, are very different in their scope. Perhaps there are no institutions which take their hue so decidedly from their teachers as schools of applied science, partly because they are fewer in number, more isolated, and therefore in closer rivalry, and partly because the field of instruction being smaller, a man possessed of unusual powers will give a much more decided cast to the studies pursued than can be the case in other schools. Among living examples of this we see Freiberg celebrated for its course of blowpipe analysis under Richter, who follows Plattner, the founder of blowpiping as a science. Weisbach, in charge of machines and surveying at the same school, and Kerl, professor of metallurgy at Berlin, also give to these places a decided character which often governs the choice of a student.

But schools have also their national characteristics, or owe their peculiar cast to the character of their founder or the object of their foundation. The school at Paris is very mathematical and scientific, following in this the bent of modern French scientific study; Freiberg, having some of the most celebrated mines and smelting-works in the world at its doors, is very practical; St. Petersburg does it best to be practical, though situated in a morass and with no mines within hundreds of miles, and it is perhaps as scientific as Paris. It combines thorough scientific training with what may be called object-teaching of the highest class. Within the precincts of the school is a very interesting model of a mine, dug in the mud of St. Petersburg, and furnished with galleries, shafts, systems of ventilation, and all the appurtenances of regular mining. The character this school has taken accords with the genius of Peter the Great, impressed upon all enterprises in Russia. He admired the achievements of science, and had experienced the benefits of practice in his own person.

The chief peculiarity of the French school is its eclectic breadth of instruction. Besides the ordinary subjects of study, the scheme there embraces, under the head of machines, such minutiæ of construction that the graduates are fitted to design machines of the greatest variety, whether for use in mines or not; and under chemistry, agricultural chemistry is taught. The reason of this is that France turns out every twelvemonth more engineers than she can employ in ten years, and in that country graduates of 1860 and earlier years still come to the offices of public works, railways, and mines, and beg for work at a thousand, five hundred francs a year, anything, in short, for the sake of employment. It is not to be inferred that these men are of second-rate ability. Their difficulty is that France has not enough mines nor works of any sort to employ a tenth of the young men who want to become engineers. Naturally enough, the schools are obliged to adopt a system of instruction so varied that their graduates shall be fitted for work of any kind. But this mingling of studies is not to be recommended in countries where larger opportunities are offered to the engineer.

French engineers, however, have an excellent reputation and find employment in all countries of the Continent, Germany, perhaps, excepted. The basis of their superior training, besides the excellent system of instruction, is in their thorough knowledge of mathematics, a study which is laid more at the foundation of engineering in France than anywhere else, unless the Russian schools are to be excepted. As before said, the Paris school is *par excellence* scientific. It has neither mines nor smelting-works ready at its hand, but this disadvantage is partly neutralized by a yearly government grant to enable a certain number of students to visit works in other countries. To such travels of the more distinguished scholars of Paris the world is indebted for a great part of its written metallurgy. The collections in this school are also very fine, among the best in the world.

At Freiberg the distinguishing feature is the opportunity for practice offered by the mines and smelting-works. The ground upon which the Saxon mining town stands is pierced by so many shafts and galleries that their united length is said to be more than five hundred English miles. They yield ore of the greatest variety. Lead, silver, and copper are the principal products of the works; but the whole number of these is said to be thirteen. Besides those just mentioned, there are gold, bismuth, zinc, arsenic, realgar, sulphuric acid, blue vitriol, and others. The works in which these numerous operations are carried on have always been celebrated as well for the energy exhibited in studying new methods as for their commercial importance. Freiberg has given its name to the best method of amalgamating silver ores, to numerous discoveries in smelting, to the Gerstenhöfer, the Pilz, and other furnaces—inventions which have altered the methods of working ores over the whole world. In former times the profit from these mines was very great. Freiberg was the royal city of Saxony, had the court, began a cathedral (of which one fine doorway now shows the promised glories), and contained sixty thousand inhabitants. At present its mines, though largely worked, yield but little profit, and its celebrity is due more to its school than to anything else. That has always maintained an excellent reputation, and its professors are and have been among the most famous men in science. The students have the advantage of practice in the mines, ore-dressing works, and smelting establishments, and, with the exception of the second of these, the practical advantages offered by Freiberg are greater than in any other school. One other thing distinguishes this academy above every other, and that is its course in blowpipe analysis—a most important subject, absolutely necessary to the engineer, but one which is singularly neglected in other European schools. Besides this, surveying, machines, assaying, and the theory of fuels are among the best treated subjects. Freiberg, more than any of its rivals, is supported by foreigners, partly because the fees required are upon a higher scale than elsewhere, and partly because it is a greater favorite among students.*

---

* The following is a list of fees for the principal studies. These fees, it should be mentioned, are the property of the professors, whose incomes are usually made up of a small fixed salary as professor, a salary as inspector, adviser, etc., in the works, and fees. The prices are given in thalers, worth 72 cents in gold, and the fee covers the course for six months:—

Mathematics, first course	20 thalers.
Mathematics, second course	20 "
Descriptive geometry	20 "
General elementary mechanics	20 "
Elementary mining mechanics	18 "
Machines, first course	10 "
Machines, second course (construction)	20 "
Theoretical surveying	15 "
Practical "	20 "
Theoretical chemistry	20 "
Practical "	25 "
Analytical "	30 "
Metallurgy, general	20 "
Metallurgy of iron	10 "
Dry assaying	30 "
Wet "	15 "
Blowpipe analysis	20 "
Mineralogy	25 "
Mineralogical practice	12 "
Crystallography	6 "
Physics	16 "
Geognosy	20 "
Lithology	12 "
Theory of veins	10 "
Practice of Petrography and Lithology	8 "

The school at Berlin is a transplantation of that at Clausthal in the Harz Mountains. Though the latter has not been given up, it has lost the professors whose labors had made it famous. Others, however, have replaced them, and the school, though its prestige has gone, is perhaps as good as ever. Dr. Von Groddeck, its director, is an able and industrious man, a good instructor, and a scientific student. Among the men who were transferred to Berlin is Kerl, the professor of metallurgy and author of a standard handbook on that subject. This school also has the services of Gustav Rose, Rammelsberg, and other men, leaders and even founders in part of the sciences they have taken up. It was established many years ago, but has only lately begun to have its present almost exclusive importance in North Germany. It is the only school of the highest class connected with an institute, all the others being independent foundations.

Although Austria has no one school where the sciences of mining and metallurgy are taught in all their length and breadth, its instruction is, nevertheless, of the best kind, but divided among three schools, each of which has its especial field of operations. To the Empress Maria Theresa of Austria belongs the honor of founding at Chemnitz in Hungary, in 1760, the first academy of mines in the world. At that early day the idea of practical

---

Mining, first course	20 thalers.
Mining, second course	20 "
Mining laws	15 "
Book-keeping	10 "
Drawing	15 "

Besides these sums there are smaller ones to be paid for the use of chemicals, instruments, etc. The school expenses of a student are perhaps about one hundred thalers a year, some paying half and some nearly double that sum. Twelve hundred thalers a year, or eight hundred and sixty-four dollars in gold, is the average expense of a student in Freiberg.

The idea of self-support does not enter into the plan of European schools of mines, which are founded for the benefit of the mining service. On the contrary, natives of the state receive compensation during their term of study on condition of entering the public service. Since the growth of the mining interest in America, however, and the presence of great numbers of our young men at foreign schools, the pay exacted from foreigners has become of great importance to some of them. At a time when the academy at Freiberg contained nearly two hundred students, not one quarter of these were Saxons intending to enter the state service. From forty-five to fifty were from the United States, and this fourth part of the students paid at least one half the fees received by the professors.

in preference to strictly scientific training, was uppermost. At Chemnitz the mines produce gold, silver, and lead ores, with all their complications, requiring the knowledge and practice of every device of metallurgy; and that school is, therefore, the metallurgical one of the three. Leoben, in Styria, is situated in the midst of the Austrian iron region, and therefore the school for the study of iron-working is situated there. At its head is Tunner, the best authority on scientific iron-working on the Continent. Pribram, in Bohemia, has very large and old mines, and within the last twenty-five years has been the field of operations of Rittinger, undoubtedly the foremost student in the art of dressing ores, and one of the most scientific of inventors. Pribram is his workshop, containing a greater variety of machines than any other similar work in the world. At the school situated here mining and ore-dressing are therefore the principal studies. To the engineer who selects mining, *per se*, as his exclusive occupation, the shops at Pribram are, perhaps, the most interesting point in Europe.

This system, formerly so esteemed, of planting the school close to the mine, and restricting its scientific character to a close correspondence with the opportunities for practical experience, is now going out of favor. Of the four principal academies in Europe, I have already shown that three are situated far from mines. Paris and St. Petersburg are so far from the mining-field that "practical courses" are impossible. Berlin has the advantage of the Clausthal mines for the training of her students in the summer months. The additional advantages offered by a great social and scientific centre make the situation of this school perhaps the best of any in Europe. The Austrian government, following the desire of all its engineers, is now considering a scheme for the union of its three schools in one academy of the first class. Austrian engineers have found themselves hampered in their practice by the too exclusive direction of their early studies to one separate division of a subject, which, however comprehensive, is still homogeneous. In point of fact, nothing could be more unfortunate than this seclusion of a school in a mining town. The studies should necessarily give a fair importance to each branch of the subject; and this cannot be done if the attention and observation of the students is concentrated on only one class of mines. A school situated over a mine does not turn out *mining engineers* in general, but coal, iron, lead, or copper workers, as the case may be. When undue importance is given to one metal or ore, the rest suffer; and no good school can find illustrations of a full course in one region. Wherever it is it will be separated from the practice of the greater part of the subject, and therefore its location defeats the very purpose of its existence. On the other hand, it was reported a year or two ago in Freiberg—on what authority it was not stated—that a commission, sent by the Berlin government to ascertain the best seat for a great school of mines for the North German Union, had reported in favor of that place. This step, if made, would be in violation of the lessons of European experience; and even if this report be true, it is still doubtful whether such a concentration of schools will ever take place. The University of Berlin would be loath to abandon so excellent a member as its *Bergakademie*, and the Prussian government is too anxious to see Berlin a "Weltstadt" to suffer one of its most important institutions to be dismembered.

Although for the number, present value, and future promise of its mines, America may be called distinctively *the* mining country of the world, it was not until 1864 that we severed the bonds of our dependence upon Europe in the matter of instruction. Up to that time we sent our young men abroad for their technical education; and on their return they brought home, not only men educated to work at particular kinds of mining, and the sectional prejudices which hamper foreign schools of mines, but too often antiquated ideas of management as well, too cumbrous for use in the American field. They copied the faults of foreign engineers; and it is safe to say that foreigners do not succeed in our mines. A German who has no knowledge of mining may succeed as well, after living here long enough to imbibe a portion of American adaptability and pluck, as an American who also knows nothing about it. But, paradoxical as it may appear, it is still true that a foreigner, who has studied at home, and is quite ready to enter an establishment there and pursue the regular round of promotion with good reputation and even distinction, will be much more likely to make a failure here than his uneducated brother who has been long enough in the country to learn American ways of working. In this remark I broach no theory, but give the general opinion of miners in the West. A few foreigners have distinguished themselves there; but an experienced miner will often prefer to trust a tyro born in America rather than a foreigner fresh from home and with all his knowledge new. And the reason of this, instead of being an argument against mining schools, is an argument for them, but for schools in the right place.

There is an inherent difference in the pure and the applied sciences, in that while the rules of the former are forever true and unchanging, the same in Europe and in America, and in India or Patagonia as well, the latter, by the very fact of their application to given circumstances, and to requirements of fixed conditions, have no immutable laws, except such as they borrow from the pure sciences. The laws of chemistry are fixed the world over; but operations in the industrial arts that succeed perfectly in England or America fail in India. Nor is distance a necessary element in this diversity. Meteorological differences, obscure variations in material, and the like, seriously affect similar operations, even when they are carried on at no great distance apart. In nothing is the diversity of nature more apparent than in the composition of the earth. The life of the mining engineer is spent in applying the principles of science to this immensely varied mass. Mines are not only very variable among themselves, but the same mine differs in its height and its depth, in its length and its breadth. By the very nature of things, the engineer must know what differences of treatment the components of this mass require. This can certainly be ascertained as well by the foreigner as by the native. But in addition to these purely scientific questions are others more embarrassing yet. There is the eternal question of profit, with its complications of wages, prices of material, transportation, etc., and often political and national characteristics, which must be understood as well. It is in this latter part of an engineer's requirements that the foreigner fails; and the greater his experience abroad the more likely is he to fail here. For mining engineering, in which term I include metallurgy and all the branches of knowledge which the conduct of mines and smelting-works demands, is not merely a special application of science to industry, but it is for each engineer a special selection of some branch of a great subject. A science that requires such strict devotion requires, too, particular instruction. Even in the beginning the student finds it advantageous to select his particular field of labor, and apply his best powers to its study.

In Europe this is true in a much higher degree. Schools there owed their foundation to the desire of perpetuating a race of men who understood, not the laws of science, but the technicalities of the particular mine or works with which the school was connected.

For the mining schools of the lowest grade were founded almost before there was any science, and when instruction was altogether practical. They have themselves been the cradles of science and research.

Much of this methodical adherence to tradition is still retained, not so much in the schools as in the works where the engineer always finishes his studies with two or three years' practice. In the first steps of his instruction he begins by wheeling a barrowful of ore; but not a step may he stir until his thumbs are in the true traditional position, where the thumbs of all miners who have gone before had rested. From the beginning his drill is like the drill of the soldier. He does everything by a fixed method, which has in it no inherent reason for being used in all places and at all times.

This cannot be done in America, and the man who has learned to rely upon fixed rules in small things, and have men about him who are accustomed to one way and one method, finds himself unable to work when he crosses the ocean. Wages, habits of work, character of workmen, all is new and everything confounds him. Engineering, like the law, consists not so much in the application of abstract principles as of good precedents to a given problem. And the trouble with a foreign engineer is that his precedents are all wrong; they cannot be applied here. Therefore, for the real welfare of our mines as well as for the dignity of our nation, it is necessary that we should have our own schools of mining science.

This necessity being conceded, the question arises, Can we introduce the foreign system entire, with its instruction for workmen of every class? Unfortunately, we cannot. The lower schools depend so closely upon practice in the works that they cannot be carried on without the consent of private owners or the establishment of government works. Both of these supports are closed to us, for the government is opposed to public works of profit, and, great as the advantage of educated workmen would be in smelting-works, there is not the least likelihood that any company, however important its operations were, would be willing to give its workmen the necessary instruction. We are, therefore, forced to build our house from the roof down—to found the mining academy at once.

It is evident that, in establishing these schools, care must be taken to restrict their number and to place them in well-chosen situations. It is well for America that experience in Europe has demonstrated the needlessness of placing the school at the mine's mouth. Here it would be impossible to obtain in a small mining community the support required to maintain expensive professorships, collections, and libraries. Such an institution needs the nourishment only to be obtained from the innumerable rills of knowledge and wealth which flow into great cities. In Europe the professors are considered as necessary to the development of the mines as the actual directors, and draw their pay from the mining department of the government; the collections are filled by the constant contributions of the mines, and all specimens which are found belong to the schools, for profit or preservation; the libraries are filled with works written by the professors and the directors of government establishments. But in America all these things must be paid for by school fees, yearly gifts, or endowments. It is far better to concentrate these supplies upon a few well-supported schools than to attempt a thousand diversions of the resources at hand, by adding a course on metallurgy or mining to each of the schools of technical science, or each of the colleges in the country. Indeed, such an addition is far from making a mining school out of these institutions. It is not merely that a school of this kind must have its lectures on mines, machines, metallurgy, mineralogy, geology, chemistry, and other subjects, but these must be made both generally complete and especially adapted to the engineer's wants. A school of mines is a great, complex, comprehensive machine, requiring many men, who all work with one and the same end in view—to fit the young engineer before them to grapple with a subject which has puzzled the wisest for centuries, and which is every day coming into closer union with all the other sciences, from meteorology to hygiene.

The problem presented to us is to establish, upon the American system of self-support, schools, with all their expensive professorships, collections, and libraries, which shall in every respect equal the foreign institutions. It is well for us that experience has proved great cities to be the proper seats for them. It is well for us that we start when science is older and the errors of our rivals have been exposed.

At present there is but one fairly established school of this class in the country—that in New York. Institutions which bear the the name of schools of mines are also to be found in New Haven, Boston, Troy, Philadelphia, Ann Arbor, and many other places.

But those where the instruction is general and complete, as at Cambridge or New Haven, lack the students necessary to form a living school, while the others have no claim to the title they have taken, except by virtue of a course of lectures on metallurgy or mining tacked on to their regular studies. The latter are no more schools of mines than is the Military Academy at West Point, where a course on metallurgy has been given for years. They lack, not only the purpose, the singleness of aim, the undivided attention to one absorbing subject without which a school of this kind has no life, but also the support necessary to carry on so expensive an institution.

The position of our mining fields is another ruling consideration both in respect to number and position of our schools. In a country covered in every part by mines, any division into districts must be arbitrary. But by taking other elements into the problem, we shall find it not so difficult to point out the limits of these fields, and the best position of the schools. These elements are distance, and what may be called the educational spirit of the different regions. Thus it is plain that the Atlantic and Pacific are too far apart to be well brought within one boundary, and the same is perhaps true of Lake Superior and the Atlantic States. But are we to make one district north and another south of Mason and Dixon's line, one east and another west of the Alleghany Mountains? Certainly not. Great as is the mining industry over all this region, far surpassing that on the Pacific side, it is almost entirely divided between coal-mining and iron-working. The training of engineers for this business should by all means be concentrated in one school, which can also with ease look after the lead-works of the Mississippi Valley and the zinc and copper industries of Pennsylvania and the South. New York is the proper place for this school. It unites the qualities of wealth, literature, and science; and by its position as the commercial centre of the country, a school there has the advantage of aid from innumerable sources. Its communication with all the Atlantic and Mississippi Valley States is also perfect; and as to cost of living, which is supposed to be so excessive in that city, a young man can study in New York, with all the high fees and cost of living, for the same sum that students spend in German country towns.*

---

* The officers of the New York School have published an estimate of a

There is nothing to prevent Lake Superior educating all its engineers in New York for years to come. It is now within forty-eight hours' travel of New York, and the peculiar necessities of its mines can be studied by men working in New York. But in the progress of the educational spirit which is sure to take place in America, the school in New York will become overcrowded. There is a limit to the number of men who can study the same subject in the same school with profit. Probably the largest class one professor can take thorough care of may be put at fifty scholars. For a three years' course, such as New York has, this gives a hundred and fifty regular students as the maximum strength of a thoroughly efficient school of mines. I may say, in passing, that fifty engineers a year would be a small supply for this country, but even this is never attained. Instruction in these schools, if well conducted, is severe, and it is a wonderful success to graduate more than twenty-five or thirty per cent. of the students. Of those who do graduate, not more than one half go into the practice of their profession, the others turning off into various channels of business. When, therefore, the educational spirit rises sufficiently high to crowd the New York school, the best disposal of the overflow would be to an institution in the Lake Superior region, which could look after both the Lake region proper and the Mississippi Valley. But until that high-tide mark is reached in New York, and the educational spirit at the Lake has risen sufficiently, any school planted there would have but a cramped existence and a limited efficiency.

As for the Pacific slope, the kind of mining and metallurgy carried on there, confined almost entirely to gold, silver, and lead ores, and the individualism of the methods, as well as the remoteness of the district, point to the necessity of a school in that part of the country. For this San Francisco is the proper place, as the centre of educational, scientific, and commercial forces on that side of the continent. The new University of California is on

---

student's expenses in New York, which is worth reproducing. It includes the yearly fee, $200, and estimates for books, instruments, apparatus, and expenses of living for thirty-five weeks, calculated upon a minimum and a maximum basis. It it as follows:

	Minimum.	Maximum.
Preparatory year	$507	$640
First "	515	655
Second "	528	670
Third "	535	682

the point of establishing such a school, and it will have some advantages over any other in this country. Though the mining interest of the Western States and Territories, with all their gold and silver, is not to be compared to that of the Atlantic half of the continent, yet the educational spirit of the people in regard to mining is much higher than anywhere else, as is shown by the eagerness with which they welcome the foundation of the new school, and by the lively expectation they have of important results from it. In the East only scientific men have participated in similar feelings toward the New York school; but in California and Nevada it is not merely the student of science, the mine owner, or the mine superintendent, but the average miner as well, who expects and desires great things from the institution—a condition of affairs which probably results from the difficulty of working complicated gold and silver ores, the long struggle to find adequate means, and the feeling that the losses in operation are still far too large.

The people of that region are, therefore, right in determining to have their own school, which shall make the peculiar needs of their mines its especial study, and shall also introduce the many remarkable innovations they have made, and which have never yet been adequately studied, in the metallurgy of gold and silver, to the knowledge of the world. The study of American metallurgy is one of the most important tasks our schools have before them. Our knowledge of metallurgical science is almost all drawn from European sources; the travels of young engineers are made in Europe, and meanwhile our own metallurgy is neglected. It is true that it is behind the foreign methods in some respects, but it is in advance in others, and at all events no general improvement can be expected until its present condition is understood and explained. But while thus giving peculiar and natural importance to their own mines, it is to be hoped that they will not neglect the study of general mining science; that they will not fail to give their school a distinct active existence, to employ the best-informed and most scientific men, and to spare no pains to make it what New York has already become, one of the best schools in the world—more scientific than Freiberg, more practical than Paris.

The school in New York was founded in 1864. Its beginning was apparently not very promising, and yet its success was really assured from the first. Placed for the first year in three or four cellars of the Columbia College buildings, its appointments were necessarily imperfect, and the difficulties in its way were very great. But in one respect its future looked bright. It was thought that the school would be considered fairly established if twelve students presented themselves. The number was twenty on the opening day, and before the year was out nearly fifty young men had joined. The next year a building for laboratories, collections, and lecture-rooms was ready, and the number of students was about ninety, increasing to one hundred and thirty the third year. Since the start, in 1864, more than three hundred young men have entered, some for the full course and some for special studies. This gives an average of fifty new pupils a year.

The course of study is now divided into five parallel divisions: mining engineering; civil engineering; metallurgy; geology, and natural history; analytical and applied chemistry. A student can pursue any one of these, and take the degree of Engineer of Mines, Civil Engineer, or Bachelor of Philosophy. The course of study occupies three years for the two former, and four years for the last degree. There is also a preparatory year for those who desire to be well grounded in the necessary elementary studies.

The construction of a school building, and the provision of apparatus, is very far from being all the work accomplished in the six years' life of this institution. The literature of the mining profession in the English language is very imperfect, and it was impossible to conduct the school in any other way than by lectures. These lectures, too, had to be very different from those delivered in German schools. There the professor not infrequently delivers a loose, often rambling, often too dry, often too agreeable lecture, the object of which, in ordinary cases, is merely to point out to the pupil what direction he should give to his studies. He is expected to go home, and, with the lecture as his guide, to pore over his books, obtaining his real information from them. The cases where the lectures of the professor are expected to be the only or principal source of knowledge are comparatively rare. Here it is very different. The lectures are sometimes all the student has. They must, therefore, be very full in fact, but also well condensed in language, or the course would become interminable. This necessity is far from being a disadvantage. The lectures delivered in New York have the value of original examinations into the sciences they discuss, and when they are published, as is to be hoped they will be in good time, the body of mining science as contained in American text-books will be very different from that possessed by any other country.

I have spoken above of the immense labor required to carry on a mining school, and the heterogeneous character of its operations. Of this the school under discussion is a good example. Where there was not a specimen, a crucible, or a furnace, six years have sufficed for the collection of seventy-five thousand specimens, illustrating geology, mineralogy, and metallurgy ; of models of furnaces, machines, crystals, geometrical sections ; of a library of three thousand volumes ; of laboratories for assay and for chemical operations, which are larger and better than those of any other mining school in the world. The value of all these must be close on two hundred thousand dollars, and the work has been enormous.* Nor can a good school be established with less labor or less expense. But the results are commensurately great. Among all the most famous schools in the world, there is not one so well supplied with apparatus, and not one where all the departments are carried on with the same equal care. Remarkable as it may seem, no school in Europe, unless that in St. Petersburg is to be excepted, can compare with this in the appointments either of its chemical or its assay laboratories.

If the other schools which are to be founded in this country are established with equal care, fifty years will see a great change for the better in American mines. The enormous losses which are to-day experienced, even in the best conducted works, and the absurdities which are perpetrated in the name of mining, will pass away with the ignorance that causes them.

---

* The cost of this school for the last five years of its existence has been $248,049, and its receipts from students $82,134. The first year, which was exceptional, cost only about $28,000, but the average payments are very nearly $50,000, and the average receipts $16,000. These figures may be studied with advantage by those who would be glad to see the country filled with schools of this kind.

www.ingramcontent.com/pod-product-compliance
Lightning Source LLC
LaVergne TN
LVHW020742120826
845150LV00010B/2358